The Appearing Act

Healing Poetry

Masha Bennett

Copyright © 2023 Masha Bennett
All rights reserved

The Sand & Sound Centre
www.sandsoundcentre.co.uk

To Mark

ACKNOWLEDGEMENTS

I am deeply grateful to my friends, teachers and colleagues who have inspired and encouraged my poetic journey over the years, in particular Alison Smith, Rhiannon Becque, Kim Rosen, members of my online community Sand, Sound & Symbol Tribe, my local creative writing group Write From the Heart, and the Pesso Boyden therapy community.

The Appearing Act

Contents

1. Contact   5
The Appearing Act   6
The Waiting Part   8
I am Both   9
Does It Matter   10
Head, Heart & Gut   12
From the Dark   13
Words Used to be Poetry   14

2. Conditioning   15
The Inner Critic   16
Heart Space   17
On Kindness   19
Be-longing   21

3. Chill
The Boy with Cold Eyes   23
Damp Chill   24
Siberian Squill   25
Echoes   26

4. Courage, Fear, Rage   27
They Were Brave   28
Solitude   30
Rage   31
How to Make Acquaintance with a Monster   32
The Necklace   33

5. Creativity, Curiosity   34
Invisible Artist   35
Reconnecting   36
How to Be a Poet   37
The Sable Black Rabbit   38

6. Compassion, Love   39
Seized by Love   40
If I Ruled the World   41
Everywhere   42
I Don't Know   43

What If	44
How to Create Healing Moments	45

7. Companions, Helpers   46
Bear Talking	47
Breakfast	48
Black River Birth	49
Fern Frond	50
I Walk with You Part of the Way	51
I Am On Your Side	52
Ideal Mother Song	53

8. Connection, Nature   55
Gratitude	56
Unbecoming	57
Two Dandelions	58
What am I looking for?	59
If My Soul	60
Grey Heron	61
How to be Awe-Some	62
Spring Has Arrived	63
Not My River	64
If I Was a Bug	65
Lines	66
The Hammer & The Lotus	67
Ode to Straw	68
New Moon	69
I Am Here (Song)	70
The Mountain	72

9. Comic Relief   73
Ode to Blue	74
Hoverfly	75
Silence of Bugs	76
Ode to Hot Water Bottle	77
Political Limericks	78
Lockdown Lament (Song)	80
Dungarees	82
The Essential Acts	83

1. Contact

The Appearing Act

Piece by piece I was stolen
My Disappearing Act
Wasn't an act of magic
Wasn't a trick, or a plan, or at all intended

Each piece, unacknowledged, unseen
Was thus taken away, vanished, forgotten
First by those with unseeing eyes, unhearing ears
Then by me, myself, mimicking the only thing I knew

I have been searching for those pieces
In an attempt to complete the puzzle
This is my Appearing Act
This is my lifetime work, in progress

I see and hear and witness
Those stolen pieces of myself
One by one
I acknowledge their invisibility
I gaze into their blank expressions
I witness their mistrust, their caution

You jolly well should be cautious, be mistrusting
I will wait here, until you are ready to come alive
Until you accept my embrace, and let me
                         paint you in glorious colours
Until you are ready to join hands and dance

No longer disappearing in a haze, vanishing
                         into a magic cabinet
Appearing, stretching to the light, still unsure, still hurting
But risking the exposure to the elements,
                         the warmth, the cool breeze
Even if just for a brief moment

Dear stolen pieces
I give you permission to retreat back into the dark,
Into the nothingness
But only if absolutely necessary

The thieves no longer have the power over you
Their script is no longer your story
Let's make a new story together -
A peculiar, unfamiliar sort of story

The one that doesn't shame and doesn't turn away
The one that is tasting life as if for the first time
The story of possibility of touching and being touched
The story of the Appearing Act and of what happens next

The Waiting Part

'O the one who withdraws
            what are you waiting for?'
'I wait for you...
to take my hand,
       walk togetherly
           our feet twinkling'
O yes do, do, let's!
giddy fireflies of our feet
     walking
        GA-LLO-PING
           tum-b-ling...
the mossy path trembling,
      the tenderness of togetherness
          shakes the Earth

I Am Both

I am both fading and I am blossoming
I am both vocal and I am mute
I am both passionate and "can't give a toss"-ing
I am both blunt and I am acute

I am both connected and disjointed
I am generous and greedy all at once
I am delighted and I am disappointed
I have a fluid and a rigid stance

I am full of anger and compassion
I am loving and indifferent - I'm both
I am logical and I am irrational
I work hard and I am full of sloth

I am fearless and I am oh so scared
I stand tall, and I am on my knees
I am defensive, and my soul is bared
I am both, and that is how it is

Does it Matter?

Does my healing matter?
Do the little changes in me
Subtle, like rice grains
Or more like molecules
Make any difference at all?

Who cares if I've worked on myself
Painstakingly, for twenty five years
That I've made limited, not so steady progress
That many of the steps were backwards,
And those that were forwards
Were shaky and unremarkable?

What does the planet gain, if anything?
From my new awarenesses, realisations
My digging around in shadowland
My reaching out to heavens
Isn't it all navel gazing?
And how long must one examine
Own bellybutton for?

Am I kinder? Am I braver?
Am I prepared to stand up for others
Or even just for myself?
Is there anything revolutionary
In my emerging understandings,
In shedding a few layers of defences?
It isn't going to feed the hungry
Or stop the destruction of the Earth

I have not invented a new medicine
Or a way to teleport, or time travel
I am a little gentler with myself, and maybe others
I am a little softer in my heart and around it
And yes I see the beauty that isn't always noticeable
And yes I speak the truth - sometimes, not always

I don't know, dear planet, if I have much to offer
But the thread of connection with other beings
Exists, and that feels sufficient, both tiny and enormous
Connecting heart to heart or hand to hand
Like branches reaching out, almost touching
Those of another tree in ancient forest
Like mycorrhiza weaving fungal wonders
Like sunbeam playing on this stone and that one

Does my healing matter?
I do not know
Perhaps it matters as much as a frog croaking
As much as a starling fluffing up his feathers
One drop of dew falling
The gust of wind lifting up
The ordinary dust of life
Perhaps it matters

Head, Heart & Gut

Where does the path lead?
Which mysteries are shimmering in the cool air
and marking your way - not anyone else's?

Follow the mysterious messengers
even if the Mind swithers
The Heart will know exactly how to love, regardless
The Gut will know exactly where this journey leads

From the Dark

My dark and your dark,
Blending together, shimmering,
Your eyes are glim-glimmering
With old, mysterious spark
Your eyebrows a questioning arc

My light and your light
One and the same, brilliant
We are two in seven billion
All light and all darkness, despite
The rules... that we shall overwrite

My breath and your breath,
Breath on this earth, momentary,
Just enough time for commentary
A poem or two before death...
A poem or two before death

This poem has evolved into a song which you can hear on my YouTube channel https://www.youtube.com/ @PracticalHappinessUK

Words Used to Be Poetry

Words used to be poetry
Now, fossilised beyond all recognition
They no longer sing
They churn out lines of data
They mumble, drearily, in foggy hesitation
They knot themselves in tongue-tied fear

Where is that dreamy melody that Words used to possess?
That sweetness and surprising sharpness,
Even shock, of rise and fall of intonation
And syllable that rides the wave of joy that fills the mouth

Words used to be poetry
Where are they now?
Please bring them back!
For rise and fall, and swirl, and dance
Of those delicious singing syllables,
A hymn for every knotted Soul
Who'd lost her poetry
And doesn't even know it

2. Conditioning

The Inner Critic

1.
My inner critic
Can rant and smirk and shout
I say, 'Sit back, chill'

2.
Peace does not last long,
The drone of the nagging voice
Alive and mocking

3.
My inner critic,
Ever ready to pounce
'Hush', I say softly

4.
'Hush', I say softly
'My friend, you seek perfection
In all wrong places'

5.
My inner critic
Relentless in her duty
Of stating all faults

6.
I embrace her stiff,
Nervous body, which trembles
And fears to let go

7.
My inner critic
Longing for beauty and peace,
Finding it nowhere

Heart Space

If my brain was as big as the Universe,
Or as small as this fungus,
Would I be smarter, or dumber than you?
And would it matter?

If my skin was paler than a translucent snowflake,
Or as dark as an over-ripe fig,
Or golden, or rainbow-coloured -
Would I be more or less beautiful than you?
And who would decide?

If I hopped on just one spindly leg,
Or shimmied along, fast, on twenty,
Or hardly moved at all,
Would I still have the right to tread on this Earth,
Just like you?

If I spoke a different tongue,
Or had no tongue at all,
If I was deathly silent, or wailing
Would I merit being heard by someone,
Maybe someone like you?

Thankfully,
Both of our hearts are as big as the Universe
Regretfully,
You are stuffing yours in a jam jar

Wait! Stop! It doesn't fit..
That Cosmic heart of yours,
Embracing all multi-coloured skins, feathers and scales
All tongues and songs as its own,
All types of leggedness and leglessness,
As parts of you and me

All our hearts hurt in pretty much the same, familiar way,
AND have capacity to love hugely, cosmically
Don't stuff yours in a jam jar
It can't breathe in there
It can't embrace and hold all there is
It can't Love as it was always intended

On Kindness

1.
'Such a kind girl', the woman gently says
The door is carried from the pathway to the porch
The girl, awash with warm glow, radiant
Grasping onto the the word, k - i - n - d
Like a glistening thread - or is it a hooked fishing line?

2.
Grandmother's tired hands, warm and cracked
Caring, carrying, cooking, darning, wiping the tears
'Be kind, be kind, be kind', the train speaks to the track
Writing out the foolproof recipe for worthiness -
Simple, and deceptively nutritious

3.
The girl peeking out of the fortress of books
Is there a broken soul out there, needing to be enveloped
And carried to safety, to love, to wholeness?
The basket is full of them, like mushrooms,
                                           she can barely lift it
But lift it and carry she does

4.
'I have just murdered someone, a woman, for money...'
'Not to worry, of course I get it, I may have
                              done the same...'
Here is a soft, round shoulder to cry on, to lean into,
A sofa, some snacks, soothing talk -
Do you want one of my eyeballs perhaps?...
'Ah how curious, a postage stamp
              with a famous dictator's profile -
Must be rare!'

5.
The morsels of appreciation are rich, warm, undeniable
They snake in and nourish the girl, feed those
                          cold cobwebby places
She's earning them hard, earnestly, breathlessly
Giving up her breath, her atoms,
                even her lovers, almost willingly
'Please, sir, I want some more?.. Some more?...
                        A little more?...'

6.
Would her bones, her blood be enough
                            in exchange? Her hair?
Maybe the lymph, the tendons? The dreams
                        she has dreamt?
The essence of her being?
The angsty poems and songs from her teenage self?
            (No, way too gloomy..)
Let's have that sweet smile, the soft wrinkles at the eyes
A self-deprecating joke or two will just do it...
What's left there to surrender for the illusion of worthiness?

Be-longing

Be-longing...
What if we could BE with our LONGING?

With ancient terror of devastation and loss
Snapping at our feet
How can we be-long?
What if we annihilate the universe
And
     ourselves
          with
               it?

Go, go, blow, do it
What needs to go, blow, like a dandelion clock -
                                    poof!
Be, be, be - in, out, and right through it
Longing for the cure for the mildly entertaining
                                    spoof

Of your real life, true life, naked with its hunger
                                and tender-ness
Be-longing in all corners of the world,
                       light and shadowy
How do we meet each other with this fear
                 and longing for together-ness?
How do we?
      How do we...
            How do we...

3. Chill
___

The Boy with Cold Eyes

Whose light is it anyway
And whose is the darkness?
Can you recognise the flickers of both
In your beingness?

Under your skin, in your salty pores,
In your tremulous heartbeat,
Can you taste that duality
That is our human-ness?

The boy whose eyes are cold,
Unseeing, unloving, unloved
Could he truly receive the warmth
Of the one Great Mother?

Outwith time, outwith space
Darkness and light are cooked
Into one delicious porridge
By Her who can nurture the boy

May the warm steam rise,
Soothe the millions of wounded souls,
Melt the shard of the mirror
Lodged in his unseeing eye

May the permafrost of his heart
Give way to first flowers of spring

Damp Chill

Damp chill
Knocking on every fibre of my body
Then, unceremoniously
Kicking in the door, laughing gleefully
And taking my whole body hostage

No amount of layers can protect me
Neither can movement
The straightjacket of chill
Penetrates the tissues with sharp hooks

My only hope
My only saviour
Is the blessed hot water bottle
She alone can battle the monster
Bit by bit
Defrosting my brittle insides

I can almost hear the ice crunching
The glassy surface of the lake of my soul showing cracks
Is it nearly spring? Not yet
But the rubbery heat of my friend makes me
                wistful, hopeful
My limbs more pliable
My eyes no longer stinging with bitterness of cold air
My teeth unclenching and some defrosted saliva
                flowing again
Like a mountain stream born of a glacier in April

Relief!
My gut no longer a bag of frozen peas and sweetcorn
My being unfurling like a soft frond from
                a melted patch of snow
I am, patiently, waiting for spring

Siberian Squill

When I was a child
I called you a "blue snowdrop"
You were the very first flower
To poke through the snow in our yard

I waited with baited breath
For this sign of life, of vitality
The sign of emerging from endless darkness
Of gloomy Moscow winter

My single blue snowdrop,
So tender, and so strong
Pushing through the crusty dome of snow
Melting the cold fortress around you

With the outbreath of spring
Stretching to the sunlight
Every April, like clockwork
You never failed me

Echoes

Fearful of a shadow
Of a near-forgotten past
That is still quite alive,
Snaking its way,
With its icy fingers
Squeezing the heart
Ever so slightly,
Whispering, 'Don't forget,
You are ssstill ourssss...'

I shake off these
Creepy tentacles,
I shout 'No! Get lost,
Don't you dare
Slither into my light,
Into my freedom!

I am standing firm
Here, now,
You are my history
And the Learnings from you
Are welcome,
The Lies and Cruelty are not,
Any longer!..'

And yet, as I embrace
These unwelcome demons,
Reluctantly,
They shed their skin,
To become Truth and Compassion,
To bring healing and grace to
Where I stand

4. Courage, Fear, Rage

They Were Brave

They were brave.
They just didn't know it
They cried and ached and feared
Like everyone does.
Or may be more

As their fluttering hearts
Were just that little more tender
Just that little more full
Of the loving potential
That was left unrequited
Or cruelly shattered

They thought, 'I am scared...
I am alone... I am small...'
They did not think 'I am brave'
But they were

They were courageous
They were full of spirit
That they carried, reluctantly, rebelliously
Through the months and the years
The decades, the centuries
Without knowing their true power

What I really want to say is:
They always were and they are brave
I would like them to know it
I want them to remember it
To feel the courage of their fluttering hearts
And the strength powering
The fibres of their muscles

The treasure chest of the brave
Contains all kinds of riches
The fear as well as the courage
The pain as well as the true spirit
The anguish as well as the joy
It is all there, sparkling with rainbow light

And I would like them to open the lid
To look at these treasures
To own them and to share them
With us all
So that we could all learn a lesson
About bravery

Solitude

Salt... Solution... Solidarity... Solid... Salubrious...
Any word beginning with the sound 'sol' - but that one
Solzhenitsyn... Solomon... Solstice... Soliloquy...
I am running out of 'sol' words

I must now turn towards the one I've been silencing
Solitude
The solo etude of my life
The music of it
The aloneness of it
And the slow, solemn dance of it

This game of solitaire hardly offers salvation
The salty, solidifying crystals where once was my heart
The mind is insolvent
The spirit is slovenly
The body soliciting touch
But someone is shouting, 'Sorry, it's all sold out!'

And the soul... the soul is just about consolable
Longing for solitude... fearing solitude...
Doing the work that the soul does best
In the soft and familiar arms
Of solitude...

Rage

'What is this unfamiliar stirring?
The hot, rumbling magma?'
'I am Rage'

'How come you arrive in the peaceful palace
Of my body?
What the hell are you doing here?'

'What the hell, indeed
I am Rage
The shouter of justice
The preacher of fairness
Yes, I am sanctimonious and sometimes unreasonable
Reasonableness is banished here, now
Merciless, outraged, outrageous
Wanting to smother the in-justice, the un-fairness
With hot smouldering wreckage of all that's familiar'

'Welcome then, come on in
Here is the chair - not fireproof, mind you
I trust you to tell the truth
To shout it
To spew the volcanic lava, if need be

I'd like to get to know you
I want to share in your energy
Your vitality
Your truth...
Our truth'

How to Make Acquaintance with a Monster

Find out where the monster lives
It may not be where you think
Existing maps may come in useful
As may a local guide with knowledge of the land

Into the monster's lair, however
You'd have to go alone
You may take a torch
But no weapons

Even if your heart is ready to jump out of your chest
Even if you are convinced that the beast is about
                              to eat you alive
Even if you are cursing the day you decided
                              to make that journey
Don't take the weapons
They may scare the monster away

'Good!' - you may shout -
'That is just what I needed!'
No, it isn't!
I can tell you for sure that peace, love and joy
Are not achieved through driving the monster away
It is part of this land, it lives here

So, take a torch, and some snacks, and some courage
And enter the monster's lair
Make an offering, even if your hands are trembling
Look into the eyes of the being
That has been giving you nightmares all this time

Look into its eyes. Listen to its heartbeat.
Notice how your hearts beat as one.
Share some snacks. Talk. Cry.
Light a campfire.
Sit together, gazing into the flames

The Necklace

A string of pearls of Consciousness -
Truth nestling with Courage
Strength huddling with Love
Wisdom together with Joy

Do I dare to wear this precious necklace?
Do I let it merge with my skin, with my being?
I am rather fond of my fake plastic beads
I am thoroughly used to them

They are colourful, shiny and reassuring
They've been made in a factory
By fellow humans, just like me
So much more understandable
Than some nebulous "god" or "divine"

I am frightened to lose the brightness, the certainty
To exchange the familiar beads
For the shimmering light of the pearls
Still unknown and maybe, terrifyingly, unknowable

Do I dare this swap?
Can I have guarantees, please?
Am I allowed to change my mind?
Or, better, can I have both?
Silence...

I am listening for the answer
In the trees, in the river
In the hum of a neighbour's strimmer
In the centre of poppy flower...

I am not finding it in any of these places
There must be another place I must look.
And tenderly listen

5. Creativity, Curiosity

Invisible Artist

I do not know since when, how or exactly why
But an unseen and playful artist must frequent this beach
When tide goes out, leaving all exposed and naked
He strides past marram grass, through sand,
                                          to water's edge
With his palette of orange, greys and creams and browns

Painstakingly, he decorates each pebble
Their stony little souls vibrating with delight
And whispering their dreams and wishes to the painter
He pours, and splashes colours
He draws the lines and dots with delicate precision

The pebbles sigh with gratitude and pleasure
And - whoosh! - the sea rolls in and swallows them again
Too eager to conceal their shameless glory
The artist vanishes into the salty air...
Until the tide goes out - then he'll be back
His paints replenished, brushes at the ready
He'll pour, and splash and draw
And decorate the stony little souls

They'll flaunt their pretty frocks to passers-by
Until the sea rolls in again
And all repeats, like it has done forever

Reconnecting

I was lost, disconnected, and barren
No words, sounds or tones slipped my breath
Whilst it may have not been apparent
That life was little better than death

My eyes barely registered colours
Even less they could notice the light
Life was empty, with that listless pallor
Dreams were vague and, at best, black and white

My body was limp, disconnected
Its movement robotic and pained
The calls of my soul were neglected
It was trapped and unfairly detained

My fingers were stiff and unsure
Unable to mould or create
The lifeless existence endured
But thank god that it wasn't too late

The bars of the prison are shattered
Grey windows of apathy cleaned
I focused on what truly mattered
And oranged, and purpled, and greened

The colours returned, and the sound
The melody danced in my heart
My feet reconnected with ground
My fingers were ready to start

To mould, or to paint, or to doodle,
To strike, or to stroke, or to strum
My lips were all set to canoodle,
To whistle, to sing, and to hum

With purpose, my soul resurrected
Her vision as sharp as a knife
I commit to be fully connected
To all that's creative in life

How to Be a Poet

Don't be a poet
Don't be anything
Don't be... it's pointless

Instead, allow an unfamiliar, tiny speck to emerge
From the darkness - that could be you -
Or, could be an acorn, a piece of gravel
An infusoria, a buzzard, or Pablo Neruda for all I know

The speck, I reckon, has a soul, the beingness
That carries poetry within it
That assaults you, engulfs you in its aliveness
Throws you back and forth mercilessly
Or caresses you intently like a touch-starved lover
Or whispers dark spells into your tired ears

Release, release the speck into the wild!
And listen, look, and smell voraciously
It comes in words, in breaths, in tremblings of the heart
In tender strokes of hand, in weird dreams,
In taste of lemon, or hazelnuts, or dust

And when the deed is done and poem is born
The labour torturous, or gentle, or ecstatic
Allow the speck to rest, back in the darkness
To brew the next concoction of the potion

Don't be a poet
Don't be anything...
Until the speck returns,
                and commandeers your essence

The Sable Black Rabbit

The Sable Black Rabbit
Leaping the Universe
Soft as darkness itself
Fierce as the essence of Fierceness

Hopping from black hole to galaxy
Through the Saturn rings
Through the gaps in the atoms
And back to black hole again

It is in the Universe, not of it
Humming to the dance of the stars
Weaving golden threads in the cracks
        between parallel worlds

Splashing in the meteor shower
Playing with the marbles of the Solar System
Munching on the Milky Way like the most
              delicious carrot
My Sable Black Rabbit

This poem was inspired by my work with Metaphors of Movement (a model developed by Andrew T Austin) and resulted from my personal exploration on the theme of 'What is my creativity like?'

6. Compassion, Love

Seized by Love

I am seized by Love
I claim no ownership
of this force,
of this ground of possibility

Community, commonality, compassion
descend on me like a flock of birds
sensing a place of readiness,
a place of nourishment

Potential for the seeds to - pop! -
fracturing the hard shell
Up they grow, and up, and up, and up
to take the space they were intended to take
Nothing more

If I Ruled the World

If I ruled the world
I would make kindness a subject in school curriculum,
I would share with the young and the old the
                      joys of compassion.
I would make the laughter wrinkles in the
                      corner of our eyes
The official symbol of grace and beauty.

I would make holding hands and hugging tightly
As normal and beautifully ordinary,
As the breeze in the trees, as the bird song, as the beam
                      of sunlight on the windowsill.

I would say to all, 'Feelings are welcome here,
And I will be with you while you feel them.'
And I would invite others to join me in this gentle mantra.

If I ruled the world
There would be much sharing,
Sharing of love, of wisdom, and other preciousness.

Everywhere

Love is everywhere
Just look
Even the hardened, crusty hearts
Long for the L-word
Grieve for what hasn't been
Dream of tenderness
Of a warm embrace

Even the cruel, the mercenary
Who built walls around their hearts -
For good reasons, usually -
Weep silently with unbearable pain
Of disconnection, of empty space
Where there should have been love
And lots of it

Love is everywhere
But we bathe ourselves in superficiality
Protect ourselves from intimacy
'Too risky!' our ancient brain declares
'Let's think about it', the neocortex proposes
'I am here', whispers the heart -
'And I long for love'

I Don't Know

I don't know the words of Truth
That would heal, repair the irreparable
Actions speak louder than words
But my arms hang limp, helpless

I don't know the words...
That would break the spell of cruelty, despair
Reaching out, I am tongue-tied, limb-tied
Quietly furious, infuriatingly silent

I don't know...
The right way to heal the world
I know it isn't my job, truly,
But may be a tiny bit of it is, after all

I don't...
Imagine that words, even of poetry
Have the power to overcome darkness
But may be they can bring
              a glimmer of light to it

I...
may not have the right words, or actions
                          just now
But I do have a big, fierce, roaring Love
May the right words and deeds be born
                      in its embrace

What If?

What if Love has always been there?

Both soft and solid, real
Speaking in a voice of tenderness
And holding with strength in its sure arms

Love that can be trusted
Ordinary and reliable

What if it has always been there?

How to Create Healing Moments

Find a space.
Four walls, floor and a ceiling kind of space
In the absence of that, trees, rocks, earth
        and sky would do very nicely.
Bring a bottle of water, cup of tea, or another beverage
That leaves your senses free to roam, unimpeded.

Make a cosy nest to rest. Leaves, moss, fluffy blankets,
Somewhere to curl up and drift away if needed.
Bring some light - torch, candle, lantern
To satisfy your curiosity when you wish to shine
        in dark corners
And illuminate the previously unseen, unknown.

Tune your ear to sound. Listen. Listen to anything
Hum of the fridge, birdsong, creak of a branch
        or a floorboard
Every sound has a potential to flow through your being
Taking what's no longer needed with it.

Invite a friend. A cat, a dog, a bear
A living soul real or imaginary
That can offer its hand, or paw, and hold you
and soothe and reassure you.

Go inside and see what's there
Anything that wants to show up, welcome it
Cry the tears, rage in fury, feel the sorrow,
        shake with terror.

Your friend is there to take care of your tender soul
Your cosy nest is ready when you need to rest
Your torch or candle can illuminate the darkness
The sounds of the world will flow around and through you
The Earth will cradle you and hold you safely.

7. Companions, Helpers

Bear Talking

'I will wait here until you're ready to come
My black shiny nose smells your hesitation
Listen to the whisper of the pine trees
Your beingness is ready to start unfolding
You and I will be as one, as intended.'

I am filled with fearfulness and longing
When will I be ready, if ever?
How will I know to lean into your strength?
The pine trees are whispering still
I'm listening, I'm grateful, and I will

Breakfast

The spider in her intricate and dewy web
Awaiting breakfast... Dignity and patience...
The glistening threads adorned with jewelled rainbows
The breeze is rocking them, like some magician's hammock

Mandala-weaving mistress, poised and still
Assumes position at the very centre
And waits... and waits... and waits...
For a beloved fly to yield to her embrace.

Black River Birch

Black River Birch -
For many years, you insisted
On being a mere twig -
Not much of a muchness

And then, suddenly, one summer
You resolved to become a tree
In the stony ground of the riverbank

Your roots worked hard to obtain sustenance
Your arms stretched, reaching out
                        for photons of light
Your trunk swelled within its papery cloak
The birds began to recognise you as a tree
And came to perch, to peck on any pesky aphid
That set up residence amongst
                        your toothy leaves

You can rest this winter
With the cold river falling from the hills
                        washing your feet
The winds tickling your swelling buds
And rustling the slivers of your bark
You will wake up in spring -
A tree, a twig no longer

Fern Frond

Is this a stairway to Heaven?
To the Underworld?
Or, to somewhere on this Earth?

The green, burgeoning Earth,
Feeding us, sheltering us,
Nurturing, despite all odds
Loving her wayward children
Just as we are

I Walk with You Part of the Way

I walk with you to that place where the treasure is hidden
One foot in front of the other, one step by tentative step
This is your path, your journey,
I am your guest in this land
I have come as a gentle companion
Or as a fierce challenger, or both

I don't know what we'll meet on our way
But I know that we'll play, and we'll cry
And we'll giggle like children
And at times, solemnly serious
We'll declare the rights or the wrongs
                    of this land, of its history

We'll redraw the boundaries on the map
We may fight a few dragons
And negotiate some crevasses
Some fiery pits
And some stinky quagmires
And continue the journey, long and weary
To the mystical cavern
Where the jewels you seek are safely
And lovingly stored

And it may not be me
Who accompanies you all the way to that place
Who celebrates the discoveries with you
You'll need other guides and companions
With the rises and falls of this surprising terrain
With the changes of landscape and weather

I'm content to be there for just a part of the journey
Holding your hand, or nudging ahead, or cautiously waiting
Or whisking out my sword to protect you from harm
Or singing, in rhythm with your breath or your heartbeat
Or tickling your soles with the softest of feathers
Saying, 'Come on, just one more step!'
I will walk with you part of the way, if you let me

I Am On Your Side

I am on your side
I am beside you
Not all around you
Not all over you
Not slithering inside
To scratch and tear at half-forgotten hurt

I am simply by your side
And you, just take your time
And I'll be with you until you know the antidote

No, you don't have to be alone
And grin and bear on your own
And even then, when I am gone
A silken golden thread will still remain
Connecting us through times and cosmic planes

Your work is hard
Your work is not in vain

Ideal Mother (Song)

Chorus:
>If I had been your Ideal Mother
>You'd see yourself through the kind eyes of another
>You'd know you are strong and beautiful and smart
>I'd say you're precious and I'd carry you in my heart

If I'd been your Ideal Mother
If I had been your Ideal Mother
You'd have a place, as safe as no other
You'd have a knowing of belonging in this world
I would say 'Welcome' and in my arms I'd you enfold

Chorus: - " - " - " _

If I'd been your Ideal Mother
If I had been your Ideal Mother
Your needs would always be a pleasure, not a bother
Your voice would be the most important sound
I'd come and soothe you, I'd always be around

Chorus: - " - " - " -

If I'd been your Ideal Mother
If I had been your Ideal Mother
I wouldn't shout, humiliate or smother
I'd give you space to play and to explore
And when you need me, I'd be there forevermore

Chorus: - " - " - " -

If I'd been your Ideal Mother
If I had been your Ideal Mother
Of course I'd be married to your Ideal Father
We would be fierce in protecting you from harm
You'd have our back up and two strong pairs of arms

Chorus: - " - " - " -

If I had been your Ideal Mother
We'd talk and laugh, and listen to each other
I would feel honoured to have brought you to this world
Your soul would know it has permission to unfold

Your soul would know it has a loving space
To blossom and to grow and to unfold

This song was inspired by the concept of the Ideal Mother from Pesso Boyden Therapy. You can hear it on my YouTube channel https://www.youtube.com/@PracticalHappinessUK

8. Connection, Nature

Gratitude

What have I done to deserve this light, this life?
Love of Mother Earth so freely given
Beauty and pain both so abundantly offered
Will I accept graciously?
Will I cower and hide,
Or bargain just for the pleasurable?

Or will I stand tall on the Earth and say
'Thank you, for everything',
Will I open my arms and embrace
The bumblebee and its sting,
The light glowing through the berberis leaf
And its vicious thorn,
The flower and its death, inevitable,
The love and the suffering?

Unbecoming

I recall that am part of this Wild,
Part of green, brown, grey, dusky-red
I could just lay here in my earthy bed
And remember the wisdom I had as a child

I could lay my cheek against the rugged skin
Of the oak, and know that we are truly one
And bathe in the streams of the evening sun
And simply let unbecoming begin

Two Dandelions

'I am afraid of letting go...'
'Me too...'
'Do we have a choice?'
'No... The wind will take all our seeds and carry them away.'
'But how will we know what will happen to them?'
'We won't...'
'That makes me sad... I hope they will land in a place of nourishment and safety... I hope they grow...'
'Some of them will.'
'Only some?
'Only some.'
'How I wish I could follow them and be sure what happens to them...'
'We can never be sure... that is why we have to just let go...'
'Just let go?... It's hard...'
'It is... but let go we must...'

The wind picks up a few more seeds and
carries them,
carries them,
carries them...

What Am I Looking For?

I don't know what I am looking for
Is it a flower spilling its fragrance, shamelessly,
                for all to imbibe?
Is it a wisp of a breeze caressing the tired skin
                of my cheek?
Is it a quarrelling chorus of jackdaws
                high in the sycamores
Or a melodious query of a love-sick blackbird?

Is it a glint of gold or silver in a plain river rock,
The way the water falls, determined, fierce over the weir?
Is it the burgundy glow of the maple leaf's splayed fingers?
Is it a dew drop perched on a feathery frond, about to fall?
The ladybird's definitive black on red, or red on black?

Is it the tiny parachuting soldiers
                of the dandelion squadron,
The pink of the red campion, the sky-blue
                of forget-me-not?
Is it the soft layer of leaf litter or moss under my feet?
All I am searching for, longing for is right here
In the bittersweet wondrousness of life

If My Soul

I never get bored of droplets of rain
On fallen leaves
If my soul flutters right now
And suddenly leaves
It would not
        have been
                in vain

Grey Heron

Grey heron is endlessly patient, still
I worry about its toes getting cold
Like I worried when I was three years old
That the earthworms were getting squished
                              on the road
That my sandpit wasn't cosy enough
                              for the sleepy toad
I feel for them, still

How to Be Awe-Some

Do you want to be awe-some?
This is your instruction manual
Do exactly as I tell you
And awe-someness will be yours
Indefinitely, forever!

Stand with your mouth agape
Staring at the first star
Just beginning to glimmer
In the Prussian Blue of the evening sky
Above the thin sliver of pinky-orange

Crouch down, fall on your knees
Watch the tadpoles wiggle in muddy pond
Gaze at the mystery of metamorphosis yet to come
Wiggle-wiggle... wiggle-wiggle... wiggle -
Isn't this the most graceful dance you've ever seen?

Bow to the mesmerising beauty
Of a dandelion, a cow parsley,
Peek at the morning sunlight
Through the hole in a leaf
Chewed by this creature or that

Attend fully to the stained glass panes
Of bluebottle wings
And her jewelled body
Revel in the intricate spiderweb
And the mastery of its weaver

Do as I say,
And you will be awe-some
You will be truly glorious
As you take in the beauty
Of this unfathomable world
Of which you are a precious atom

Spring Has Arrived

When the creamy blooms of Akebia open
showing off their unexpected purple centres

When the pond is brimming over with spawn,
the love-children of randy frogs

When the furry bottom of queen bumblebee bobs,
                                  business-like,
from daffodil to primrose,
from lungwort to coltsfoot

When the sky is so translucent blue
it takes my breath away
That's when I know for sure spring has arrived

Not My River

I didn't know your name
Like I still don't know my own
Looking out from a steep patch of grass
Framed by untidy privet
Onto your vast existence

Reflecting ordinary greyish sky
Too deep, too moving, too spacious
I loved you in the way I didn't love myself
With trepidation, awe, excitement
Filling my expectant toes with wonder
To dip or not to dip?

You could have been *my* river
I could have drank you, drenched in you
And drowned
But I wasn't ready
Our encounter, though brief, carried my longing
Into a different dimension

And there, another river
A tamer, quieter and smaller sister
Entered my world, as a mere trickle
Another river tugging at my senses
Under a green canopy of tree mothers

I still remember your magnificent expanse
And thank you for the gift of non-becoming
Thank you for not becoming my river, then

If I Was a Bug

If I was a bug
I would live happily in this tree crevice
Nibbling on the toadstool, this side or that
Marvelling at the algal artwork adorning the walls
Splashing in the leafy pool, full of mysteries
Sleeping tight in the cosiest nooks of my abode
Dreaming of warm summer

Lines

Lines on a petal
Guiding a diligent bee to hidden nectar

Lines on a leaf
Criss-crossing the green terrain, carrying life

Lines on a zebra
Camouflaging her among tall swooshing grasses

Lines on a page
Where I hastily scribble the swarm of words

Lines on my face
Telling the story of life, full of surprises and love

The Hammer & the Lotus

[To the tune of 'If I Had a Hammer']

If I was a hammer
I'd hammer in the morning
I'd hammer in the evening
I'd build a solid home
All people are invited
Whatever is your yearning
The fire will be burning
You will not be alone

If I was a lotus
I'd grow in swampy ground
My fragrance would astound
I would be soft and still
My roots will anchor firmly
My flowers will abound
Imbibing sacred sound
Of water, wind and hills

Ode to Straw

A while ago you were grass
Standing tall in the fields
Bending with the winds
Playing with the sunlight
In droplets of dew

A while ago you were a seedling
Pushing up through the earth
Greeting the light and the air
And the clouds and the bird song

A while ago you were a seed
Falling into earth and resting there
In your soft dark bed
Waiting to imbibe the precious moisture
And begin the journey up into the light

A while ago you were a pollen
And an egg, coming together
In a curious embrace of plant love

A while ago
A while ago
A while ago
You were nothingness exploding
Into atoms in the Big Bang

New Moon

Baby Moon sleeping in tree branches
Leaning into the folds of crinkly bark
The end of the crescent holding onto a twig
Like a child grasping its mother's finger

Baby Moon slipping from the tree's embrace
Rolling out into the open sodalite-blue sky
Still so young and sliver-like
And powered by the magic of the Cosmos

I Am Here (Song)

I am here
I am here
Like the bark on the tree
Like the foam in the sea
I am here
Where else would I be?
Where else would I be?

I am here
I am here
Like the stream, like the heron
Like the earth, like the heaven
I am here
Where else would I be?
Where else would I be?

    Watch the sunbeam or a caterpillar grazing
    Hear raindrops or the ferny frond unfold
    It's a gift, that's why we often call it present
    We are only given moments in this world

I am here
I am here
Like the badger, like the bear
Like the blackbird, I am not there
I am here
Where else would I be?
Where else would I be?

I am here
I am here
Like the sand, like the boulder
Here's my hand and here's my shoulder
I am here,
Where else would I be?
Where else would I be?

Watch the sunbeam or a caterpillar grazing
Hear raindrops or the ferny frond unfold
It's a gift, that's why we often call it present
We are only given moments in this world

I am here
I am here
Like a smile, like a tear
Just for a moment I am here
On this earth,
Where else would I be?
Where else would I be?
Where else would I be?

This song was inspired by some of my personal work with Gestalt Therapy. You can hear it on my YouTube channel
https://www.youtube.com/@PracticalHappinessUK

The Mountain

Buttocks vast like a mountain
Rooted in the deep layers of Earth
Reaching down to the fiery magma,
And the central iron core

My body rises through the mists
Through the airstreams and soft clouds
My breath kissing the passing birds
My hair platted with rainbows

The deep rumble of my heart
Makes the rocky outcrops tremble
And then - stillness, tenderness
In between the heartbeats

My eyes, grey-blue mountain lakes
Giving birth to waterfalls of delight
Looking up towards the dark starry Cosmos
Seeing all the way back
To the beginnings of this Universe

9. Comic Relief

Ode to Blue

Blue of the sky - uplifting and gentle.
Blue of the ocean - mysterious, deep.
Baby blue is a bit sentimental.
Oh, and blue of the eyes that weep...

Blue haze of the distant mountain.
Bluebottle buzzing around.
At the back of the fridge - astounding! -
Blue mould on the cheese I have found

Blue is the throat chakra.
Blue is sometimes my mood.
I don't much like mackerel,
But can't find another rhyme that is good

Hoverfly

Hoverfly, hovering haplessly over hogweed...
'How can I help you?' the humble flower whispers
'Hummus? Halloumi? Hotdog?'
'Hmm, to be honest, honly honeyful H_2O would help...'
'Here it is, hun...'
'Hurray, heaven is here!' hums the hoverfly,
                              happy, hiccuping...

Silence of Bugs

Flies buzz
Bumblebees drone
Dragonflies hum
Then, the sounds are gone...

Silence of ladybirds
Silence of greenfly
Silence of mantises
Silence of lacewings

I stare right into a butterfly's eyes
In hope for a beautiful sonic surprise
The butterfly quietly sipping on nectar
As solemnly silent as a ghostly spectre

I may hope for a rousing cry from an ant
To be honest somehow I suspect that he can't
I've gone as far as acquiring a human louse
It happily sucks blood but is as quiet as a mouse

Maybe they talk but we do not hear
Maybe not enough sensitivity in my ear
They may be singing a merry song
Maybe my senses are getting it wrong
They may be performing rousing speeches
Or stand up comedy that would leave me in stitches

Silence of earwigs
Silence of shield bugs
Silence of stick insects
Silence of mayflies
Silence
Silence
Silence...

Ode to Hot Water Bottle

Oh glorious H W Bottle,
Could I live without you?
Could my fingers and toes avoid hypothermia
            without your warmth and protection?
Is there anything else that would soothe
            and comfort like you?
Emphatic 'No' reverberating through the Universe!

I shower you with rosebuds,
I pray for your immortality - or at least a
            respectable old age, without leaks!
I kiss you, inhaling the sweet rubbery smell
(You could do with a wash, if only
I could let go of you on this bitterly cold, snowy day)

Political Limericks

Priti Patel

There was a young lady called Priti
Whose thoughts and whose deeds were not pretty
Compassion she lacked
As she yelled, 'Send them back!'
And I can't even say nothing witty

Katie Hopkins

There was a young woman called Kate
Who made good excuses for hate
When hate came and bit
Out her dummy she spit
And so did J Clarkson, her mate

Suella Braverman

There was a young lady, Suella,
Whose policy was a bestseller
'UN laws we shall ditch,
Refugees will be stitched!'
All in all, her compassion was stellar

Dominic Raab

There was a young fellow called Dom
Who presented himself with aplomb
Though manners he lacked
He escaped being sacked
But, alas, his career has bombed

Nadine Dorris

There was a young woman Nadine,
For the peerage she craved and she preened
Rishi ducked and he swerved
As she screamed 'I deserve!!!'
Never seen we a scene so obscene

Lockdown Lament (Song)

[To the tune of the folk song 'P is for Paddy']

As I went out one May morning
To take my daily walk
Two policemen appeared at my side
And gave me an official talk

They said I have exceeded my
Allocation for exercise
So I now had to pay a massive fine
And go home and stay inside

Chorus:
     Oh, quarantine has stuffed us up
     Can't turn no left, no right
     While Boris & Co. do what the fuck they want
     And it seems there is no end in sight

I went to buy some groceries
I really hoped I could
I put on my mask and cleaned my hands
I tried to be so effing good

There were empty shelves where bread should be
No eggs or toilet roll
So I queued for an hour to get one carrot
And a beer, and it gladdened my soul

Chorus: - " - " - " -

Bonnie postman brought a parcel
From Amazon from Prime
I have bought two hundred DVDs
As I've watched all Netflix dozen times

My neighbour grassed me up again
He spied my bonnie postman wave
In return I refused to bring a cake
To his next illegal rave

Chorus: - " - " - " -

Anti-vaxxer friend has chided me
'Beware of Bill Gates,
He will put a tracker in your arm
And beam you into outer space!'

I've had my vaccination now
Had to rest one day in bed
Had a few unpleasant side effects..
And, thank goodness, haven't grown an extra head...
Yet...

Chorus: - " - " - " -

You can hear this song on my YouTube channel
https://www.youtube.com/@PracticalHappinessUK

Dungarees

Lifetime ambition
Has come to fruition
Who needs degrees
When you can have dungarees?!

I can never tire
Of this splendid attire
Some have cars or rockets
I have FIVE denim pockets!

The Essential Acts

Dozing deliberately and
                          diligently

Resting radically, with
                          resilience and resolve

Lolling about languidly,
                          lusciously, lovingly

Contemplating the cat
                          canoodling with your calf

Napping naughtily, whether
                          nefariously nude or not

Messing around, in a mesmerising manner,
                          or mundane

Faffing about frivolously, and furiously,
                          and doing fuck all

Sleeping solidly till the sunbeam shines its
                    softness onto the skin of your shoulder

All these are the essential acts

About the author

Masha Bennett's poems touch into the themes of human conditioning, connection, creativity, compassion, courage and other topics of healing, self-realisation and personal development.

She is a UK-based trauma-informed psychotherapist working creatively with metaphor, symbols, sandplay, art, clay, nature and Pesso Boyden therapy. Her Sand & Sound Centre is a hub of creative therapy and training in Stockport, Manchester https://sandsoundcentre.co.uk.

Masha lives in the High Peak with her partner, two dogs and a cat. This is her first poetry collection.

Copyright © 2023 Masha Bennett
All rights reserved